EXECUTIVE TIME MANAGEMENT

Philip Marvin

An AMA Survey Report

A Division of American Management Associations

Library of Congress Cataloging in Publication Data

Marvin, Philip Roger, 1916-
    Executive time management.

    (An AMA survey report)
    1. Time allocation surveys--United States.
2. Executives--United States. 3. Industrial manage-
ment--United States. I. Title. II. Series:
American Management Associations.   AMA survey report.
HF5500.3.U54M38   658.4'093   80-17658
ISBN 0-8144-3140-2

CONTENTS

Highlights and Conclusions   1

1. The Manager's Day   3

2. Dividing the Time   7

3. The Management Workspan   15

4. A Do-It-Yourself Time Analysis   19

   Appendix: Profile of the Survey Participants   25

EXHIBITS

1. How Managers Divide Their Time Acting as Managers, Specialists, and Mentors   4

2. How Managers Allocate Their Time to Various Activities   8

3. How Managers Distribute Their Time Among Nine Management Functions   10

4. How Managers Divide Time Spent Innovating   12

5. How Managers Prioritize Their Time   13

6. Percentage of Time That Could Be Eliminated Without Loss of Effectiveness   14

7. How Frequently Managers Arrive Early   15

8. Why Managers Arrive Early   16

9. Why Managers Work Late   16

10. Managers Reporting Business-Related Evening Obligations   17

11. Time Analysis Worksheet of a Hypothetical Respondent   20

12. Time Analysis Worksheet   22

13. Time Analysis Worksheet Showing Average Percentages of All Respondents   23

14. Distribution of Respondents by Size of Company (Number of Employees)   26

15. Distribution of Respondents by Industry   26

16. Distribution of Respondents by Salary Range   27

17. Distribution of Respondents by Number of Years Worked for Present Employer   28

18. Distribution of Respondents by Number of Years in Present Job   29

ABOUT the AUTHOR

Dr. Philip Marvin is currently professor of professional development and business administration at the University of Cincinnati. His career includes work as a corporate executive, researcher, consultant, author, and lecturer.

From 1965 to 1973, Dr. Marvin was dean of professional development at the University of Cincinnati, prior to which time he was president of Clark, Cooper, Field, and Wohl. Earlier he was a vice president and director of Commonwealth Engineering and a director of Basic Research, Inc. He also served as director of research and development at Penn Control's Milwaukee division and a director of engineering at Bendix Aviation.

Dr. Marvin has acted as a consultant to American Telephone and Telegraph, Johnson and Johnson, Corning, ASME, NASA, General Foods, International Minerals, 3M, and American-Standard. He has served on the international committee of the American Society for Public Administration, and has traveled and lectured extensively in the field of business education. Dr. Marvin has written 14 books in the field of management, and over 75 of his articles have appeared in this country, in Europe, and in Japan.

Dr. Marvin holds an engineering degree from the Rensselaer Polytechnic Institute, a doctorate in business administration from Indiana University, and an LL.B from LaSalle. He is also a graduate of the Oak Ridge Institute of Nuclear Studies.

ACKNOWLEDGMENTS

The author wishes to thank the survey participants who so generously gave of their time in completing the questionnaire. I am also grateful to the members of the AMA team of professionals for their advice and support. Mr. William Newton merits special recognition for his assistance in preparing the questionnaire.

HIGHLIGHTS and CONCLUSIONS

A manager's day is a sequence of responses—to the telephone, the in-basket, the appointment pad, the conference room. Each response tests his ability to control time.

How do managers occupy their time on the job? What 1,369 managers do with their days is revealed in this survey report. For the first time, a definitive picture of a manager's day is portrayed, from the time he walks into the office until the last piece of after-hours paperwork is placed in the out-basket. The managers themselves speak out—sometimes bitterly—on efficiency, time conflicts, and counterproductive activities.

Of the managers surveyed, 208 (or 15 percent) were chief executive officers, 359 (or 26 percent) were vice presidents, 733 (or 54 percent) were general managers/managers, and the rest, 69 (or 5 percent) were supervisors. Organizations ranged in size from over 25,000 employees to under 50, with the majority of managers (57 percent) representing organizations of 751 to 10,000 employees.

For many members of this group, the days are very long: most arrive before formal hours, and half of the presidents and vice presidents stay in the office 30 minutes to an hour or longer after closing. But, on the average, only *47 percent of their working time is taken up with managerial activities.*

What happens during the other 53 percent of the day? "Most managers spend their time *doing* as opposed to managing," according to one respondent. The doing might involve anything from contacting customers and making sales calls to working in an area of technical specialty. This is shirt-sleeve time spent with the machinery that makes the business go, and it consumes an average 31 percent of the manager's day. Much of the remaining time is spent showing others how to do things—the mentor role.

Which management functions require the most attention? Planning and decision making take up a combined 38 percent of management time. Concern with staffing receives the smallest portion. One interesting correlation emerges: all managers—from supervisors to chief executives—distribute management functions in very much the same manner, regardless of level.

Time allocations change when more of the day is devoted to the management role. Time spent in decision making increases drastically, as does time devoted to activities labeled "essential" and "supporting."

Some managers appear to be racing against the stop watch. Catch-up work, entertaining, and travel encroach on the hours many would devote to family or personal interests. Many do not take their full allotment of vacation days.

Who works the hardest? If this question can be answered by looking at the amount of time spent on company-related matters, the answer is quite clear: the presidents.

When asked to assess the efficiency of their

time utilization, the respondents formed two camps. Nearly half (45 percent) said they could make no reduction in working time without losing effectiveness. The other half (55 percent) said that they could reduce their time by an average 23 percent. A small but significant 9 percent said they could eliminate *over 40 percent* of their working time without loss of effectiveness. They admit that much of this time is spent on tasks unrelated to company goals or on activities that are useless or counter-productive. One general manager observed:

"Eighty percent of our time is spent on trivia, 20 percent on meat and potatoes."

A single activity can be examined from many points of view: the role the participant plays, the degree of efficiency, the urgency of action, the impact the event will have on the company's future. The present survey was designed to put time into perspective through such multiple-focus analysis. An event is not a two-dimensional object, like a picture drawn on paper. Only when viewed from several perspectives—top, bottom, and sideways—does it have dimension and depth.

1

THE MANAGER'S DAY

The makeup of the manager's day is more often misunderstood than viewed in proper perspective. Having the title *manager* doesn't mean that the working day is spent managing.

According to the 1,369 managers who participated in this survey, only 47 percent of their average working day involved management activities. And, the portion devoted to management time varied among management levels. Supervisors reported they spent 39 percent of their time managing; general managers/managers devoted 44 percent of their workdays to managing; vice presidents spent 49 percent; and presidents allocated 60 percent of their time to management matters (Exhibit 1).

Looked at from a different perspective, these managers are allocating more than half their working hours to nonmanagement activities. This is not to suggest that these activities are of lesser importance. The intent here is not to make value judgments, but to understand how time is deployed at different levels in the organization.

The averages for all managers showed that 31 percent of their time is involved in specialist or *doing* time—in other words, technologist time.

This is certainly understandable. Managers don't start as managers; they start as technologists, doers. Those who display a willingness to do what they are told to do and an ability to do things right are assigned increasing responsibility.

According to a president: "Managers appear to have one common fault; they retreat to functional activity with which they are more comfortable." A vice president added: "Most managers were promoted because of superior performance in a technical area and continue to function as experts rather than managers." Another manager commented: "Most managers spend their time doing as opposed to managing."

Gradually in moving from the specialist/technologist role, managers also assume a third role: training, counseling, and appraising subordinates—in other words, serving as mentors. Survey respondents reported 16 percent of their time was involved in training, counseling, and performance evaluation.

All three roles are essential to getting things done.

SPECIALIST/TECHNOLOGIST ROLE: 31% OF A MANAGER'S TIME

The specialist/technologist role is the most decisive role in the careers of managers because it determines whether they will ever play other roles. In any activity people must take small steps before they are permitted bigger ones. Accountants must perform satisfactorily on accounting assignments before they manage other accountants. Sales managers must sell before they manage those who sell. Engineers must be contributing members of a project team

EXHIBIT 1: How Managers Divide Their Time Acting as Managers, Specialists, and Mentors.

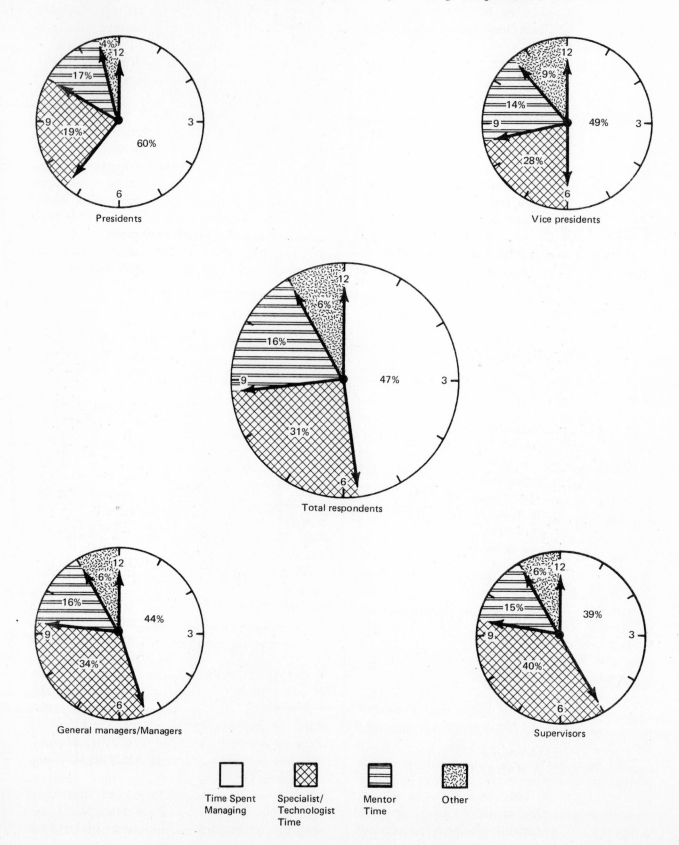

before they can be project managers. Those who are outstanding as doers are selected to manage others. Those who do not measure up are left behind.

Less obvious is another aspect. Those who turn in top performance as specialists/technologists are better managers of their own activities; they *managed* to do a better job.

It is often argued that outstanding performance as a functional specialist—say, an accountant or engineer or research investigator or police officer—is no indication of the ability to manage others. On the surface this may appear valid, but the issue demands further examination.

There is a reason why some do a better job than others. Some develop their abilities to a higher degree. Some put their skills to work in areas that produce lesser and, therefore, more manageable frustrations. Some do a better job of matching tasks to available skills.

Outstanding performance is evidence of the ability to manage personal resources. Thus, top performance as a specialist/technologist reflects a degree of management skill.

Nevertheless, outstanding performance in the role of specialist/technologist does not itself indicate a desire to move into management. Many choose to remain auditors or architects or research chemists. The role is important because by doing, a person becomes familiar with the details that provide a basis for decision making skills used later as a manager. Without this familiarity, the individual can't identify opportunities to do more worthwhile things in more worthwhile ways.

Specialist/technologist time varied among management levels. Supervisors reported 40 percent specialist/technologist time, the highest figure for the categories surveyed. Then in decreasing order, general managers/managers reported 34 percent; vice presidents, 28 percent; and presidents, 19 percent.

THE MANAGER'S ROLE:
47% OF A MANAGER'S TIME

The "I am the boss" role is the controlling role. Managers play manager roles *only* when they identify worthwhile things to do; develop plans for doing these things; organize the resources required to deliver what's wanted, with time and costs calculated in advance; staff programs; assign authority for the exercise of initiative; fix accountability for achievement; review operations; and realign programs as required.

Recognition that managers relinquish their managerial role when they play other roles is essential to understanding the nature of the action taking place. Management roles go unattended while managers return to their earlier, more familiar technologist roles, which they know how to do better and faster than the newcomers who took their place.

Then, too, output offers security. Managers can develop a sense of insecurity because they produce few tangible products. The computer specialist or tax expert or research authority says, "I'll no longer know more about the technology than my colleagues do if I don't spend time as a technologist." This is true. Moving toward management entails moving from specialist to generalist.

Some managers find it more comfortable to do than to delegate. Others are workaholics for whom long hours are equated with success. For others, the economics of the situation may dictate that they play more than one role. They may make sales calls, do the buying, or design the product when the organization has no full-time sales representative, buyer, or designer.

THE MENTOR ROLE:
16% OF A MANAGER'S TIME

Portions of the working day are taken up with such activities as showing others how to do things, helping others to solve problems, sharing experiences, and evaluating performance.

Important as these things may be, they are positioned apart from specialist/technologist and management time. Inevitably, managers who have moved up from functional specialists are called upon to act as advisors, coaches, trainers, and evaluators passing on a legacy of skills and functional knowledge.

However, mentor activities can become a time trap, particularly when managers aren't aware of how much time is taken up by these activities. When too much time is absorbed in mentor activities, some restructuring is in order.

The variation in mentor time among the four managerial levels, unlike management and specialist/technologist time, did not reveal a pattern or trend. Supervisors reported 15 percent mentor time, general managers/managers, 16 percent; vice presidents, 14 percent; and presidents, 17 percent.

THE JUDGMENTAL ASPECT

No one can presume to tell managers how their time should be divided among the three categories. Time and circumstances determine that allocation.

However, managers operate in a competitive environment where doing the most worthwhile things in the most worthwhile ways is essential for those wishing to maintain a leadership posture.

Identifying and controlling the circumstances that surround the doing of these things never ends. This management role is neglected at a manager's risk.

2

DIVIDING the TIME

Managers manage the time of their lives: 1,440 minutes each day, wisely or foolishly. Time cannot be expanded or compressed. It is a resource that once lost cannot be replaced.

Although the allotment of time cannot be increased, the rate of return can be multiplied. To do this, managers must gain some perspective on where time is spent.

Survey respondents were asked to examine their time from different perspectives. First, they were asked to indicate, in rough percentages, the amount of time allocated to various situations: planned activities, routines, customer-initiated responses, emergencies, and government requirements. Next, they were asked to distribute time spent in actual management among nine management functions: decision making, planning, organizing, delegating, staffing, implementing, evaluating, controlling, and innovating. Then information on various types of innovation was requested. Finally, the respondents were asked to assign time percentages to categories ranked in importance from "absolutely essential" to "counterproductive."

Each question called for a shift in point of view. The answers provide four perspectives for examining—and evaluating—how time is spent.

RESPONSES TO SITUATIONS

One manager responds to situations as they arise; another deals with matters by defining priorities. Some persons seem to be continuously coping with emergencies; others live predictable and routine lives.

The 1,369 respondents to this survey reported that 44 percent of their time was allocated to planned activities, 27 percent to routine work, 14 percent to customer-initiated activities, 12 percent to emergencies, and 11 percent to government demands (Exhibit 2).

The various levels of managers showed no significant differences in time taken up by routines. Presidents and vice presidents spent slightly more time with planned activities; and as one might expect, supervisors and managers spent more time coping with customer-initiated requests. In time spent handling emergencies and responding to government regulations, supervisors again reported a higher figure.

The most productive time is planned time dealing with priorities. Although emergencies are unforeseen occurrences that command immediate attention, putting out fires can leave a manager no further ahead at the end of the day than at the start. Managers who are primarily firefighters are forgotten as soon as the flames die down and the builders take over.

MANAGEMENT FUNCTIONS

Exhibit 3 shows the nine concurrent functions cited as essential to effective management,

EXHIBIT 2: How Managers Allocate Their Time to Various Activities.*

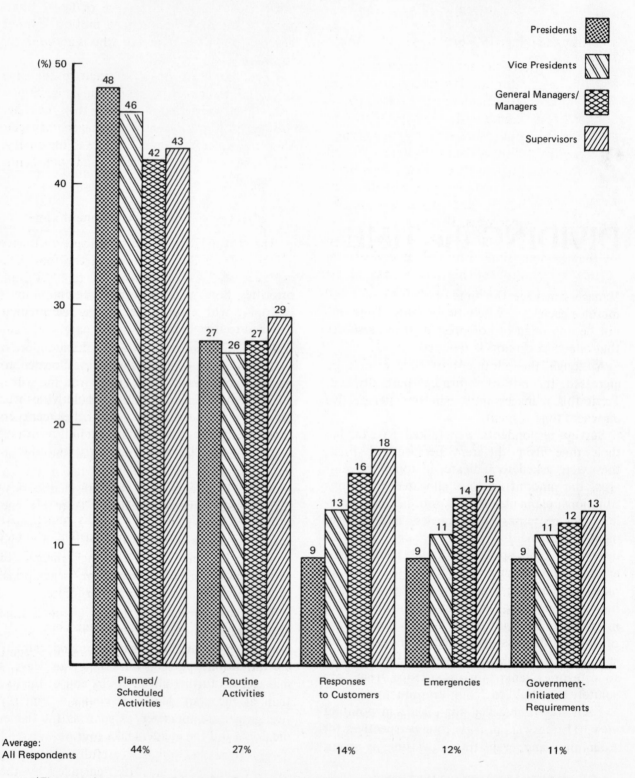

| Average: All Respondents | 44% | 27% | 14% | 12% | 11% |

*The categories are not mutually exclusive. Consequently, the percentage totals for each management level exceed 100 percent.

along with the percentages of management time for each of the four categories of respondents.

Decision Making: 19% of Management Time

Decisions direct the action. The process starts with the search for and identification of things to do and involves calculating the consequences of each action. It ends with a commitment.

Presidents spend more of their management time making decisions than any other function. They allocate 23 percent of their management time to decision making; vice presidents reported 20 percent; and general managers/managers and supervisors, 18 percent.

Remember, of course, these are percentages of management time. For the supervisor who spends 40 percent of his day managing, the amount of decision making time translates into about half an hour. For the president, the time almost doubles. Still, this is a healthy indication that decision making is practiced at all levels of management. Although the gravity of the decisions may differ, it's clear that all managers see themselves as taking part in the decision making process.

Planning: 19% of Management Time

The respondents on the average spent as much time planning as making decisions: 19 percent. Although there were minor variations among the four categories of respondents, on the average, managers/general managers allocated more time to planning than to any of the other functions.

According to one manager, "Planning time is my most effective time. I walk each activity through my mind in several ways, spot the possible problems, select the optimum alternative, and decide what I'll do if troubles are encountered along the way. Then I can delegate with confidence. It takes time, but it frees more time than it takes."

Planning has been defined in many ways, but "walking each activity through in advance of the action" is one of the best ways to explain what planning is about.

Organizing: 13% of Management Time

In the absence of a well-developed organization and a well-understood structure, people move independently and more or less haphazardly. Plans can't be put into motion without defining who does what and who is accountable to whom.

Organizing took up 13 percent of the time the total respondents spent managing. Supervisors spent more time organizing than the other managerial levels; general managers/managers allocated 13 percent of their time to organizing; vice presidents, 12 percent; and presidents, 11 percent.

Delegating: 12% of Management Time

The survey revealed no significant difference in the average time managers in the four categories allocated to delegating: 12 to 13 percent. However, two weaknesses in the process of delegation were cited repeatedly by respondents. One was an unwillingness to part with any significant segment of the workload. "We're doers when we should be delegators," wrote one manager. "The majority of managers waste half of their time on details that could have been delegated," wrote another. The other weakness cited was delegation of accountability without delegating the authority to carry out the assigned tasks.

In a very real sense, delegation is generic to the management process: a person isn't managing when he performs the tasks himself. Although effective delegation transfers a degree of autonomy in scheduling and executing the assignment, ultimate responsibility for results remains with the person who delegates.

Staffing: 7% of Management Time

One respondent stated, "My most important job is to be sure that each of those who report to me is a perfect fit for the job. When my subordinates are qualified, I have time to do my job rather than their jobs."

Managers can eliminate many problems if they analyze each job area carefully, identifying the key proficiency factors demanded by the assignment, and searching out those best qualified by skills and temperament for that job.

The survey showed that supervisors allocated

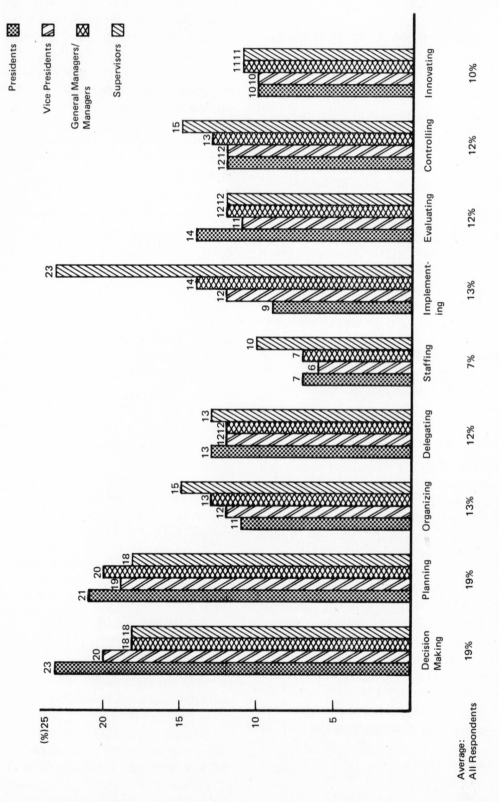

EXHIBIT 3: How Managers Distribute Their Time Among Nine Management Functions.*

Presidents

Vice Presidents

General Managers/
Managers

Supervisors

	Decision Making	Planning	Organizing	Delegating	Staffing	Implementing	Evaluating	Controlling	Innovating
Average: All Respondents	19%	19%	13%	12%	7%	13%	12%	12%	10%

*The categories are not mutually exclusive. Consequently, the percentage totals for each management level exceed 100 percent.

more time to staffing (10 percent) than managers in other categories did. General managers/ managers, vice presidents, and presidents reported they spent 6 to 7 percent of their time staffing.

Implementing: 13% of Management Time

Not surprisingly, supervisors, those closest to the firing line, spent the greatest amount of their management time (23 percent) implementing. General managers/managers reported 14 percent; vice presidents, 12 percent; and presidents, 9 percent.

Many managers overlook two fundamental facts. First, implementation problems arise because other management roles are neglected. Second, implementation problems will recur until adequate attention is given to the causes of the problems. Decision making, planning, organizing, and staffing set the stage. Managers who allocate a disproportionate amount of time to getting things going, telling persons what to do and how to do it, and keeping things moving are probably not concentrating enough on their other responsibilities.

Evaluating: 12% of Management Time

Presidents spent more time (14 percent) evaluating than any of the other managers, who reported they devoted 11 to 12 percent of their time to this activity.

Failure to audit the action has been the downfall of many a manager. Audits are a key management input, because they tell managers what is happening while it is happening. Reports tell managers what has happened, not what *is* happening. Furthermore, when managers audit the action, subordinates are motivated to do more because they know their contributions are recognized.

Controlling: 12% of Management Time

Supervisors reported the highest percentage of time allocated to controlling activities: 15 percent. The time of those in other management categories was 12 to 13 percent.

The two traditional fundamentals of management control are to *expect* and to *inspect.* A third should be added: to *correct.* Managers must follow through and initiate corrective action when the action is going on. Calling a subordinate into the office to talk about last month's performance is poor management practice. To act effectively, a manager must know what people are doing, how they are doing it, and how it relates to performance standards for the assignment.

Innovating: 10% of Management Time

New ideas can change the course of an established business. An office boy's suggestion that the hole be placed in the point of the needle rather than at the other end revolutionized the sewing machine industry. For years, Coca-Cola could be served only at soda fountains because the syrup had to be mixed with carbonated water before it could be served. The suggestion, "bottle it," gave an entirely new dimension to the soft drink industry.

Opportunities to do new things can be found everywhere, from the entry level to the boardroom. And the best way to get from the entry level to the boardroom is to search for innovative solutions. But, as one manager pointed out, "Finding better ways of doing what you're doing isn't worthwhile when what you're doing isn't worth doing anyway." Innovation demands an eye for what is truly worthwhile. The survey respondents allocated 10 percent of their management time to innovative action. Exhibit 4 shows the six areas that make up this portion of their time, along with the average percentages of innovative time devoted to each.

With management attention to these areas varying only from 21 percent for improvement programming to 15 percent for cost cutting, it is apparent that each innovative action receives significant attention. Moreover, the survey revealed no significant variations among the various managerial levels. For example, vice presidents reported 21 percent of innovative time was allocated to new ventures, while presidents reported 17 percent. However, because respondents were referring to fractions of the 10 percent of all management time allocated to innovative action, the difference is minor.

EXHIBIT 4: How Managers Divide Time Spent Innovating.*

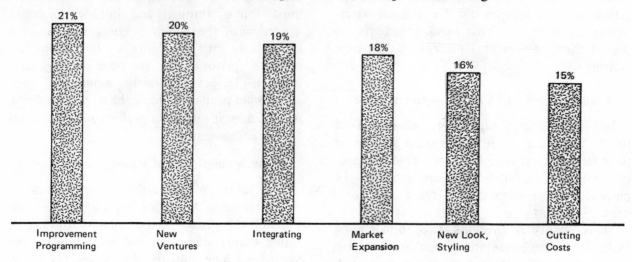

*The categories are not mutually exclusive. Consequently, the total exceeds 100 percent.

EFFICIENCY

Two questions addressed this topic. First, the respondents were asked to estimate percentages of time spent on activities ranked from "essential" to "counterproductive." Next, they were asked to estimate what percentage of their time, if any, they could have eliminated without losing effectiveness. These questions evoked the largest number of write-in responses from survey participants.

How well do managers use their time? One general manager stated, "By observing myself as well as others in our organization, I estimate 15 to 20 percent productivity." Another added, "Much of the day is devoted to nonproductive, personal tasks." A significant number of respondents commented on time wasted because of poor communications and poorly organized meetings. The most cynical evaluation came from a general manager, "Eighty percent of our time is spent on trivia, 20 percent on meat and potatoes."

Exhibit 5 shows the average percentages allocated to activities labeled "essential," "supporting," "useful," "interesting, but without tie-in to goals," "unimportant," and "counterproductive."

An activity rated as essential is crucial to the attainment of a goal. While no sharp distinction can be made between *essential* and *supporting*, a supporting activity is something that can be delayed or postponed. An essential activity cannot.

Activities classified as "useful" might include meeting people, knowing what others are doing, or reading literature in different fields. These contribute to one's effectiveness. On the other hand, an activity classified as "interesting" might be something of great personal value, but totally unrelated to the company's goals.

An unimportant activity is a time filler—small talk or self-imposed trivia that serves no identifiable purpose, personal or otherwise. A counterproductive activity not only lacks purpose, but has a negative impact.

Certainly, the categories overlap. A "useful" activity might be both "essential" and "supporting"; a time filler could be both "unimportant" and "counterproductive." This overlapping creates some difficulty in interpreting the survey data because the percentages for each management level total more than 100.

On the one hand, the survey concludes that managers spend as much as 76 percent of their time in "essential" and "supporting" activities—an indication that time management is quite

EXHIBIT 5: How Managers Prioritize Their Time.*

	Essential Activities	Supporting Activities	Useful Activities	Interesting Activities Without Tie-in to Goals	Unimportant Activities	Counterproductive Activities
Average: All Respondents	38%	37%	13%	9%	7%	7%

Presidents
Vice Presidents
General Managers/Managers
Supervisors

*The categories are not mutually exclusive. Consequently, the percentage totals for each management level exceed 100 percent.

13

EXHIBIT 6: Percentage of Time That Could Be Eliminated Without Loss of Effectiveness.

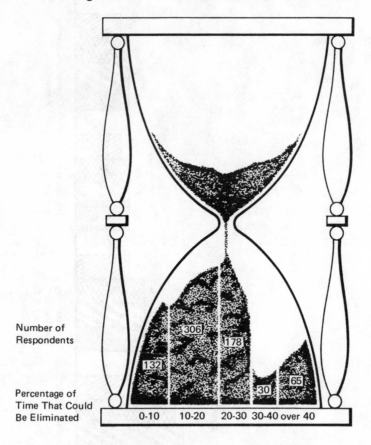

Number of Respondents

Percentage of Time That Could Be Eliminated

0-10	10-20	20-30	30-40	over 40
132	306	178	30	65

efficient. On the other, it concludes that as much as 23 percent of management time is frittered away on matters that have no relationship to company goals, are unimportant, or frankly counterproductive.

Answers to the next survey question provide the key to the data. Asked if they could reduce direct involvement on the job without losing effectiveness, 55 percent of the respondents answered "yes," and 45 percent answered "no." In other words, slightly less than half of the respondents said they could not reduce their time without losing effectiveness. These are the managers who see themselves as spending the greater part of the day in "essential" and "supporting" activities.

The other half (55 percent) make an alarming self-disclosure; they could reduce their time by an average 23 percent without losing anything (Exhibit 6). Ninety-five respondents said they could reduce their involvement by 30 percent or more.

These persons are very much aware that they do not use the 1,440 minutes of each day well. Cross tabulations in the data revealed a critical syndrome: a low percentage of the day spent on management, a great deal of precious energy expended on emergencies or responses to customer-initiated requests, and a sense that a large portion of the workday is nonproductive—as much as 20 or 30 percent. One president spoke out, "Most of our time is spent with short-range projects, and with putting out fires." A vice president wrote that most of his time was spent responding to situations over which he had no control. Several reacted to busywork that involved little planning or thinking. "We get swamped in details . . . and lose sight of the big picture."

One president summed it up. "The single difference between mediocre and outstanding managers is their efficiency in using time." The survey shows just that.

3

THE MANAGEMENT WORKSPAN

Does your workday dovetail with the pattern most frequently reported by survey respondents? If so, your formal office hours are 8 A.M. to 5 P.M. (36 percent of the respondents). For 17 percent, the formal hours were 8 A.M. to 4:30 P.M.; and for another 17 percent, formal hours were 8:30 A.M. to 5 P.M.

The 8-to-5 day was reported by 44 percent of the presidents, 35 percent of the vice presidents, and 37 percent of the general managers/managers. Only 17 percent of the supervisors, however, worked from 8 to 5; instead, 30 percent reported formal hours of 8 A.M. to 4:30 P.M.

EARLY ARRIVAL

The majority of respondents (53 percent) arrive early with some degree of regularity, and 61 percent arrive 30 minutes to an hour in advance of the formal office opening. Moreover, 41 percent arrive before their superiors, and 47 percent arrive before their subordinates. A breakdown of these figures by management levels appears in Exhibit 7.

Of these managers, 56 percent reported arriving early "to review, schedule, and plan their day." The reason, for 37 percent, was "to catch up on extra work." Other reasons for reporting ahead of formal office hours and a breakdown of percentages by managerial category appear in Exhibit 8. Sixty-nine percent of total respon-

EXHIBIT 7: How Frequently Managers Arrive Early.

	All Respondents	Presidents	Vice Presidents	General Managers/ Managers	Supervisors
	(%)	(%)	(%)	(%)	(%)
Arrive early regularly	53	49	51	55	54
Arrive early a couple of times a week	19	18	17	20	20
Arrive 30-60 minutes in advance of formal office opening	61	66	59	62	52
Arrive before supervisors regularly	41	16	43	46	49
Arrive before subordinates regularly	47	40	48	51	42

dents further reported that they believed it important to set an example for their subordinates. Only 6 percent, however, said they felt under pressure to arrive early or stay late.

EXHIBIT 8: Why Managers Arrive Early.

Reasons	All Respondents (%)	Presidents (%)	Vice Presidents (%)	General Managers/ Managers (%)	Supervisors (%)
Commuting conveniences	23.0	12.4	22.1	25.5	22.7
To catch up on extra work	37.0	40.0	37.1	36.9	28.8
To do extra professional reading	13.0	11.2	12.4	13.2	12.1
To relax and get ready for the day	17.0	10.0	13.4	19.3	21.2
To review, schedule, and plan the day	56.0	52.4	54.4	58.0	57.6
Because I work best in the morning	19.0	23.5	22.1	16.5	16.7

LATE DEPARTURE

The majority of the respondents (57 percent) reported working regularly after formal office hours. By management level, the figures are: presidents, 62 percent; vice presidents, 62 percent; general managers/managers, 53 percent; and supervisors, 45 percent.

The majority in each of these groupings works 30 minutes to an hour after the office closes—57 percent of the presidents 60 percent of the vice presidents, 61 percent of the general managers/managers, and 55 percent of the supervisors.

The reasons given most often were "to catch up on extra work" and "just to keep up with the workload." Reviewing and planning for the next day were also cited by a significant number. Other reasons are shown in Exhibit 9.

Managers reported that only on occasion do they leave before their superiors. By management level the figures are: presidents, 21 percent; vice presidents, 77 percent; general managers/ managers, 72 percent; and supervisors, 80 percent.

EXHIBIT 9: Why Managers Work Late.

Reasons	All Respondents (%)	Presidents (%)	Vice Presidents (%)	General Managers/ Managers (%)	Supervisors (%)
Commuting convenience	15.0	13.1	15.2	15.4	13.8
To catch up on extra work	51.8	47.2	50.6	52.5	64.6
To do extra professional reading	17.3	22.1	17.8	16.3	10.8
Just to keep up with the workload	45.1	50.8	49.7	41.9	38.5
To review and plan the next day	24.3	25.6	19.8	25.1	35.4
Because I work best in the evenings	8.6	6.5	8.6	8.7	13.8

EVENING OBLIGATIONS

The majority of respondents reported evening obligations extending beyond office time. By management level the figures are: presidents, 94 percent; vice presidents, 90 percent; general managers/managers, 74 percent; and supervisors, 61 percent.

The nature of these evening commitments and the percentages of managers regularly participating in such activities are shown in Exhibit 10.

Weekend and holiday work, ranging in frequency from "occasional" to "regular," was reported by 62 percent of the presidents, 52 percent of the vice presidents, 49 percent of the general managers/managers, and 51 percent of the supervisors. The remainder reported "rarely" to "never."

As to taking work home evenings, weekends, and holidays, 35 percent of the presidents reported that this was a regular practice while 29 percent of the vice presidents, 11 percent of the general manager/manager group, and one percent of the supervisors reported taking work home regularly.

Fully 60 percent of the presidents together with 47 percent of the vice presidents, 33 percent of the general managers/managers, and 22 percent of the supervisors reported that they did not take full advantage of their allotted vacation and leave days.

WORKSPAN AND MANAGEMENT TIME

Cross-tabulations between time spent in management and other data reveal some interesting correlations. Indeed, management styles differ greatly, with some executives spending less than 10 percent of the workday in a management role, and others devoting over 90 percent. Other time allocations shift significantly with increased management time.

Those persons spending minimum time managing (the "10 percent" managers) rated decision making at 16 percent. The "90 percent" managers gave decision making a 34 percent allocation. This is a significant increase in percentage of management time and a drastic increase in actual minutes.

Time allotted to planned, essential, and supporting activities showed a parallel increase as percentage of management time increased. The portion of time spent with staffing, however, diminished.

Who is the most productive? Indeed, if planned activities that are essential for the company are the most valuable, then those managers devoting the greater percentage of the day to management functions are significantly more productive. Data from those questions designed to assess efficiency support this hypothesis. The more time spent in management, the less time can be eliminated.

At the same time, the days remain very long. There is an increase in travel time and after-hours entertainment as management time in-

EXHIBIT 10: Managers Reporting Business-Related Evening Obligations.

Obligations	Total Respondents (%)	Presidents (%)	Vice Presidents (%)	General Managers/ Managers (%)	Supervisors (%)
After-hours meetings with clients/customers/colleages	73	79	74	71	66
After-hours entertainment of clients/customers	54	77	59	44	34
Evening travel to arrive for morning appointments	78	86	78	77	51
Evening attendance at public functions	73	89	80	64	56

creases. Many take work home in the evening and spend some hours on weekends and holidays in the office.

Although the increase in management time should result in less time coping with emergencies, it doesn't. This percentage remained constant across all management time groups.

Who has the longest workspan? Who runs the greatest risk of becoming a workaholic? The presidents. Twenty-seven percent reported working an hour and a half or *longer* after office hours. Fifty-two percent take work home regularly or often; 60 percent do not take their full vacation. In each case, these are the highest percentages for any management level.

4

A DO-IT-YOURSELF TIME ANALYSIS

Time is a finite, irreplaceable resource. Yet many people make the mistake of counting their money but not their time. By putting this survey to work, managers can multiply their effectiveness through time analysis. The Time Analysis Worksheet in Exhibit 11 provides a five-way focus on working time. Its simple format and step-by-step sequence imposes a minimum of intrusion during the working day.

STEP 1: RECORDING THE ACTION

Only the first two columns of the worksheet are used during the day to record the action. Recording should begin with the time of arrival, noted in column 1. The nature of the first activity should be noted in column 2. "Had a cup of coffee," or "talked with Mary about her vacation plans," or "read morning mail."

Entries should be brief but explicit. You aren't writing to anyone but yourself. Later on, when you analyze the action, your entries in the activity column should be specific enough to remind you of the details of a telephone call, a discussion, or a meeting.

STEP 2: CALCULATING ELAPSED TIME

Step 2 is taken at any time after the day's work is over. This step calls for simple sequential subtraction of entries in column 1, the clock-time column. For example, referring to the hypothetical entries in Exhibit 11, the respondent read mail from 8:25 until G.J. called at 8:40, or 15 minutes. This figure is noted in the elapsed-time column opposite the entry, "read mail."

Elapsed time should be calculated for each entry in the activity column. These figures form the basis for time analysis in the five areas of role, function, impact, urgency, and importance. In each area, the entire day's allocation of time is examined from a different perspective.

This five-way focus allows the manager to make value judgments as to the relative worthwhileness of the way time has been allocated. These value judgments will serve as a basis for improving time utilization.

STEP 3: THE FIVE-WAY FOCUS

Recognizing Roles (Area 1)

A manager rarely plays a manager's role throughout the day, although sometimes it's difficult to distinguish the roles. One manager may show subordinates how to perform a job he did before moving up in the company; another manager might attend a sales meeting for the purpose of appraising and advising the sales staff; or he might take a customer out to lunch to discuss a technical problem.

Chapter 1 on "The Manager's Day" will help distinguish the roles. As a general rule, something done on an earlier job should probably be regarded as specialist time.

Time allocations can be divided on the worksheet. For example, the 80-minute lunch with a customer might be allocated as 30 minutes

EXHIBIT 11: Time Analysis Worksheet of a Hypothetical Respondent.

Clock Time (Minutes)	Activity	Elapsed Time (Minutes)	Area 1: Role			Area 2: Management Function									Area 3: Impact						Area 4: Urgency					Area 5: Importance					
			Management Time	Specialist or "Doing" Time	Training, Counseling, Appraising (Mentor Time)	Decision Making	Planning	Organizing	Delegating	Staffing	Implementing	Evaluating	Controlling	Innovating	New Ventures	New Styling	Improvement Programming	Market Expansion	Cutting Costs	Integrating	Emergencies	Planned Priorities	Routine Activities	Customer-Initiated Activities	Government-Initiated Activities	Essential Activities	Supporting Activities	Useful Activities	Interesting Activities	Unimportant Activities	Counterproductive Activities
8:25	read mail	15	15																			15					15				
8:40	G.J.-production	10		10									10						10		10					10					
8:50	plating room	10		10									10						10		10						10				
9:00	product research	150	150			30								120	150							150				75	75				
11:30	dictation	30	30															30				30					30				
12:00	lunch with customer	80		30														30				80					80				
1:20	read mail	20	20																			20					20				
1:40	dictation	20	20																			20					20				
2:00	sales meeting	120			120													120				120				60	60				
4:00	personnel problem	35	35							35											35					35					
4:35	design change	15		15									15			15					15					15					
4:50	signed letters	20	20								20											20					20				
5:10	personnel problem	20	20							20											20					20					
5:30	left office																														
	Total minutes allocated	545	310	65	120	30				55	20		35	120	150	15		150	20		90	455				215	330				

20

specialist time, and 50 minutes management time. Other combinations are possible.

Focusing on Functions (Area 2)

The nine concurrent functions cited as essential to effective management, as discussed in Chapter 2, make up the column headings for this portion of the do-it-yourself time analysis. Again, it should be emphasized that there are no right and wrong answers. The time allocations in Exhibit 11 merely show how one person might have categorized his activity.

Focusing on Impact (Area 3)

The next area is the impact of the action in which time is classified by the expected end product of the action.

In our hypothetical case, two and a half hours involved activities related to new venture programs, and another two and a half hours were spent on related market expansion programs. These were the major concerns of the day. In addition, 15 minutes were spent on a styling matter and 20 minutes on a cost-cutting matter.

Over three hours are not accounted for here. Why not? Fifty minutes of lunch time were not distributed as business time; neither the 105 minutes spent on correspondence nor the 55 minutes spent on a personnel problem is pertinent to this part of the analysis of the day's activities.

Focusing on the Urgency of the Action (Area 4)

Why did the hypothetical respondent do *what* he did *when* he did? "It was an emergency," he might say. "It had to be done." Or perhaps, "With the tax deadline approaching, what else could I do?"

In the distribution shown in Area 4, an hour and a half was occupied with emergencies, whereas over seven and a half hours were spent doing things that had been planned.

The experience of highly effective managers indicates that when 70 percent or more of the working day is occupied with doing the things they planned to do, they have achieved a high level of control over business time.

Focusing on the Importance of the Action (Area 5)

Judgments of what is important are based on relative measures. The benchmarks for those measures are a matter of expected achievement.

The analysis in Area 5 shows that nearly four hours were occupied in activities essential to the achievement of expectations, and five and a half hours were occupied in supporting activities. Such a record would be the envy of many managers.

MULTIPLYING MANAGEMENT EFFECTIVENESS

The Time Analysis Worksheet lets the managers record and identify things they can do to multiply effectiveness. For example, the hypothetical manager has been quite effective in allocating time for priorities, essentials, and supporting tasks. But he hasn't set aside time to check up on things going on—that is, to audit the action—nor has he designated time for planning. Both columns are blank.

This poses a problem. Where could time for these activities come from? Since no part of the action can be classified as unimportant or counterproductive, trade-offs are necessary.

Deciding what could be eliminated calls for both an examination of a single day's worksheet and for a broader look at activities over a longer period—in the perspective of expected targets and goals.

The sales meeting took two hours. Depending upon the person's overall responsibilities, this individual might be assigning too high a priority to sales activities. There are alternatives. This person might limit involvement to the organizational aspects of selling and leave implementation of programs to those directly responsible. This would free time for a closer check on other ongoing activities and for planning. Following this course would have freed an hour or more of the day.

Only by disciplining themselves to make quantitative and qualitative analyses of their time can managers develop a better insight into their use of management time. There is no

EXHIBIT 12: Time Analysis Worksheet.

Clock Time (Minutes)	Activity	Elapsed Time (Minutes)	Management Time	Specialist or "Doing" Time	Training, Counseling, Appraising (Mentor Time)	Decision Making	Planning	Organizing	Delegating	Staffing	Implementing	Evaluating	Controlling	Innovating	New Ventures	New Styling	Improvement Programming	Market Expansion	Cutting Costs	Integrating	Emergencies	Planned Priorities	Routine Activities	Customer-Initiated Activities	Government-Initiated Activities	Essential Activities	Supporting Activities	Useful Activities	Interesting Activities	Unimportant Activities	Counterproductive Activities
			Area 1: Role			Area 2: Management Function									Area 3: Impact						Area 4: Urgency					Area 5: Importance					
	Total minutes allocated																														

EXHIBIT 13: Time Analysis Worksheet Showing Average Percentages of All Respondents.*

	Role			Function									Urgency					Importance					
	Management Time	Specialist or "Doing" Time	Training, Counseling, Appraising	Decision Making	Planning	Organizing	Delegating	Staffing	Implementing	Evaluating	Controlling	Innovating	Emergencies	Planned Priorities	Routine Activities	Customer-Initiated Activities	Government-Initiated Activities	Essential Activities	Supporting Activities	Useful Activities	Interesting Activities	Unimportant Activities	Counterproductive Activities
Total respondents	47	31	16	19	19	13	12	7	13	12	12	10	12	44	27	14	11	38	37	13	9	7	7
Presidents	60	19	17	23	21	11	13	7	9	14	12	10	9	48	27	9	9	37	39	14	9	7	7
Vice presidents	49	28	14	20	19	12	12	6	12	11	12	10	11	46	26	13	11	36	38	14	9	7	7
General managers/ managers	44	34	16	18	20	13	12	7	14	12	13	11	14	42	27	16	12	37	37	13	9	7	7
Supervisors	39	40	15	18	18	15	13	10	23	12	15	11	15	43	29	18	13	47	32	11	7	6	6

*The categories are not mutually exclusive. Consequently, the percentage totals for each management level exceed 100 percent.

23

better way to do this than through periodic audits using a Time Analysis Worksheet.

In doing this, the manager may wish to tailor the worksheet to his or her individual needs, adding or deleting areas for analysis and categories within those areas to make them applicable to specialized activities.

Exhibit 12 presents a blank Time Analysis Worksheet which may be copied for personal use. Exhibit 13 shows, for reference, the average percentages of time reported by the survey respondents.

More than 1,000 managers have shown how they allocate their work time. Here you can compare your own working patterns with the patterns of others, and learn from their experience.

Appendix

PROFILE of the SURVEY PARTICIPANTS

What is the makeup of the 1,369 managers who participated in this study? Who are they? What industries do they represent? The answers to these and other questions are to be found in this profile.

Size of the organization was assessed on the basis of number of employees. The majority of managers represented medium-sized companies: 32 percent came from firms employing 2,001 to 10,000 workers, and 26 percent represented companies with 751 to 2,000 persons (see Exhibit 14). Over half of the respondents (56 percent) were employed by industries engaged in manufacturing. Exhibit 15 shows the percentage distribution by industry for each level of management.

The average salary for all respondents was in the $25,000 to $50,000 range. Salaries topped $100,000 for over half of the presidents, and 14 percent received over $200,000. The average salary for vice presidents fell in the $25,000-75,000 range. The average for the general managers/managers was in the $25,000-50,000 category (Exhibit 16).

Information was also gathered on the number of years each respondent had been employed by his present company, on the length of time in his present job, on educational achievement, and on the number of subordinates directly supervised.

PRESIDENTS

There were 208 presidents, constituting 15 percent of the respondents. Seven percent held doctorates; 31 percent terminated formal training with a master's degree; and 53 percent had an undergraduate degree. Nine percent completed their formal education with high school.

While 19 percent of the presidents had no more than five subordinates, 58 percent had six to ten subordinates, and 23 percent had more than ten persons in a direct reporting relationship.

Particularly revealing was the fact that 76 percent of the presidents had been with their current organization for over ten years; 11 percent for six to ten years, and 13 percent for five years or less (see Exhibit 17).

Review of their years on the job reveals that 25 percent of the presidents had occupied their present position for over ten years, 24 percent for six to ten years, and 42 percent for one to five years (see Exhibit 18).

VICE PRESIDENTS

There were 359 vice presidents among the respondents, constituting 26 percent of the total. The formal training for 6 percent ended with a doctorate, 38 percent terminated with a

EXHIBIT 14: Distribution of Respondents by Size of Company (Number of Employees).

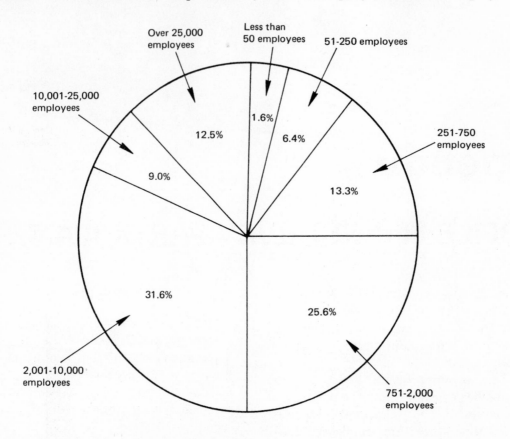

EXHIBIT 15: Distribution of Respondents by Industry.

Industry Classification	All Respondents (%)	Presidents (%)	Vice Presidents (%)	General Managers/ Managers (%)	Supervisors (%)
Manufacturing	55.8	59.2	51.7	57.3	50.7
Finance/insurance/ real estate	8.6	13.9	14.3	4.5	7.3
Wholesale/retail trade	4.7	4.3	5.9	4.6	—
Government/ military	3.8	2.4	0.8	5.0	10.2
Education/nonprofit	2.6	1.0	2.5	2.9	5.8
Transportation	2.4	1.4	3.6	1.9	4.3
Energy/mining/ chemicals	4.5	4.8	3.6	4.6	5.8
Utilities	4.3	2.9	3.9	4.4	10.2
Services	9.1	7.7	7.3	10.8	4.3
Other	4.2	2.4	6.4	4.0	1.4

EXHIBIT 16: Distribution of Respondents by Salary Range.

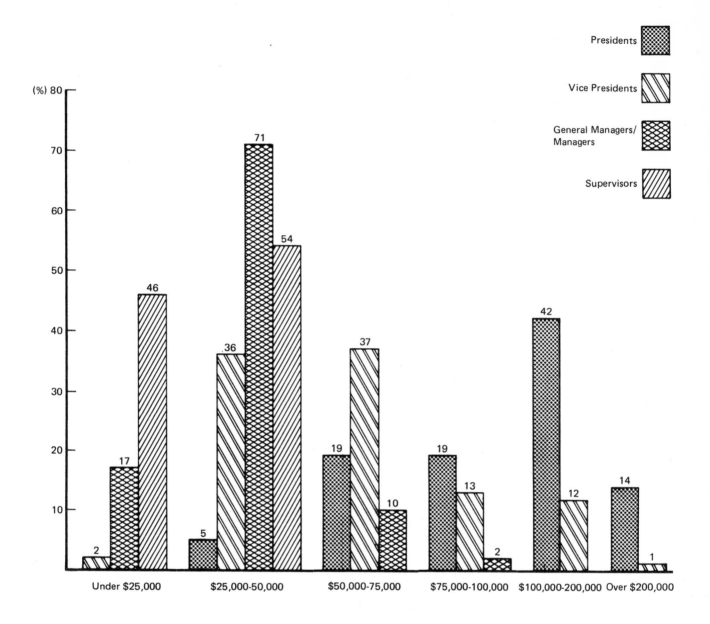

master's degree, and 49 percent held undergraduate degrees. Seven percent of the vice presidents completed their formal education with a high school diploma.

While 39 percent of the vice presidents had five or fewer subordinates, 49 percent had six to ten subordinates, and 21 percent had more than ten subordinates in a direct reporting relationship.

Like presidents, the majority of the vice presidents, 59 percent, had been with their

current employers for over ten years, 20 percent had been with their current organizations for six to ten years, 20 percent for one to five years, and one percent for less than one year.

Review of their years on the job reveals 18 percent of the vice presidents as having been in their present positions for over ten years, 21 percent for six to ten years, and 51 percent for one to five years. The remaining 10 percent of the vice presidents had been on their present jobs for less than one year.

EXHIBIT 17: Distribution of Respondents by Number of Years Worked for Present Employer.

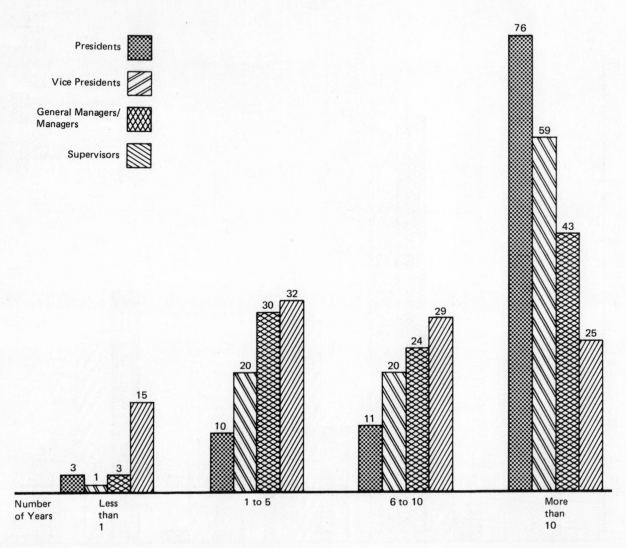

Percentage of Respondents

Presidents

Vice Presidents

General Managers/
Managers

Supervisors

GENERAL MANAGERS/MANAGERS

This management level was represented by 733 respondents, 54 percent of the total. The formal training for 6 percent of these managers included a doctorate and 34 percent a master's degree. An undergraduate degree represented the terminal point for 50 percent, and 10 percent stopped with a high school diploma.

Of these respondents, 46 percent had five or fewer subordinates in a direct reporting relationship, 29 percent had six to ten sub-ordinates, and 25 percent had more than ten.

More than ten years with their current employer was the longevity record for 43 percent of those reporting; 24 percent had been with their current employer for six to ten years, 30 percent for one to five years, and 3 percent for less than one year.

The majority of these managers, 58 percent, had held their present position for one to five years, 16 percent for less than one year, and 16 percent for six to ten years. The remainder reported having more than ten years in their current capacity.

EXHIBIT 18: Distribution of Respondents by Number of Years in Present Job.

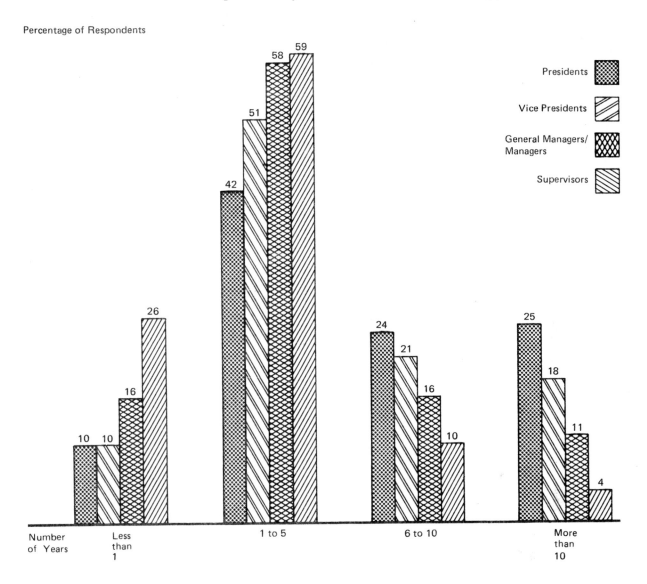

Percentage of Respondents

Presidents

Vice Presidents

General Managers/
Managers

Supervisors

Number of Years — Less than 1 — 1 to 5 — 6 to 10 — More than 10

SUPERVISORS

There were 69 supervisors among the respondents, representing 5 percent of the total. The formal training for 4 percent included a doctorate; 39 percent terminated their education with a master's degree, 46 percent with an undergraduate degree, and the remainder with a high school diploma.

In all, 59 percent of the supervisors had five or fewer subordinates in a direct reporting relationship, and 24 percent reported six to ten subordinates.

A one- to five-year service record with their current organizations was reported by 32 percent of the supervisors, 29 percent reported service of six to ten years, and 25 percent had been with their current employer for over ten years. The remainder reported service records of less than one year.

The majority of these supervisors, 59 percent, had held their present positions for one to five years, 26 percent for less than one year, and 10 percent for six to ten years. The remaining respondents reported having served for over ten years in their current capacity.